*A Mother's Journey through*

# Autism, Redemption, *and* Freedom

D1519331

Juliana Clark

ISBN 978-1-64559-357-7 (Paperback)
ISBN 978-1-64559-358-4 (Digital)

Covenant Books, Inc.
11661 Hwy 707
Murrells Inlet, SC 29576
www.covenantbooks.com

To my loves: Lillian, Paige, Noah, and Ellie,
~May your faith always be bigger than your fear
All things are possible with Jesus

IN LOVING MEMORY OF
The Believer, a man who walked by faith and faith alone
who continues to dwell in the house of the Lord forever.
For I was once lost and am now found.

# Background

From the time I was old enough to remember, I remember attending church every Sunday with my family. For several generations on my mother's side of the family, the women have faithfully attended church. I myself was raised Catholic. I attended regular mass as well as Sunday school and catechism classes from an early age with my parents and siblings. As a child, I felt very close to the Lord. I helped with Sunday school and looked forward to absorbing the many stories from the Bible. Often when I was younger, I thought about the life of a nun and what that might look like. I remember praying often as a child and feeling a sense of closeness and security from above.

As many years passed, I found myself working or making excuses why I couldn't attend church services. I still made it to church for the big holidays and important dates. I remembered stories from class; however, nothing seemed to resonate within me. I found myself bored at church paying more attention to the people around me. I found myself counting how many ladies had worn a hat to coordinate with their fancy Sunday outfits. I felt like I was more or less going through the motions or the routine of stand up, sit down, kneel than actually listening to the message the priest was professing.

Now, don't get me wrong, I was a teenager at the time and not necessarily open to hearing the word of the Lord. I believed the stories I had heard; however, I had never really dug any deeper or tried to further my faith or knowledge.

I remember meeting many people through my late teens and early twenties whom believed a wide variety of different beliefs. I began searching or rather seeking religion of all kinds trying to decipher what higher calling their must be in life. I read books of worshiping mother earth, psychic interpretations or views of the afterlife, and even attended a few tarot card readings. Needless to say, none of those avenues made me feel any sense of direction or understanding of a higher power or purpose on this earth. In fact, in looking back, I'd say it further confused me and left me feeling somewhat empty on my journey.

For several years, I enjoyed the night life, friends, and attending college. I tend to look at this time as my drifting phase through life. I was trying to find my place in the world. I met many different types of people throughout these years. Looking back, I realize I had absolutely no sense of direction or how to decipher a healthy relationship from an unhealthy relationship. I found myself let down by relationships and people in general. I can honestly say during this time, I am not sure how much I actually had to offer or give in a relationship. I was becoming hard in my views to the world around me.

Throughout college, I felt very passionate about my studies and knew I wanted to work with people on their road to recovery. I felt the need to make a difference in others around me. I felt compassionate about children, adults, and all those who were going through recovery or a diagnosis holding them back in their lives. From a young age, I attended occupational therapy services with my family. I was not the recipient of therapy; however, I was able to witness first-hand how important and vital therapy is for an individual that may be underdeveloped for their age or not meeting their milestones. I received an associate's degree of science in 2006 and graduated as an occupational therapy assistant.

This is where my life took an unexpected turn, marriage. I met my husband one month before graduating from college. I was set-up on a blind date, little did I know this would be the man I would share my life with. The plans I had of moving to a bigger city and furthering my education had been stopped short.

When my husband proposed, and we started discussing where our nuptials would take place, I remember telling him I would rather elope than have a big church wedding. My husband was also raised Catholic and even though he no longer attended regularly, he wanted the big catholic wedding. Although that is not what I would have chosen at the time, I respected my soon to be husband's wishes and began planning a big catholic wedding with our families. And of course, with any catholic wedding comes marital classes and meeting with the priest.

I remember feeling nervous and somewhat overwhelmed with attending a class with other couples also set to wed. The class was much more relaxed than I had initially anticipated, and no-one asked any overly personal questions or anything to make me squirm in my seat. I remember leaving the couples daily retreat feeling relaxed with no worry about marriage. We met with the priest and took a compatibility test of sorts, which we both scored very high on. I look back and realize I had no idea or plans of how I would incorporate faith in my marriage or what that would look like. The day of our wedding, I felt a presence while standing at the altar while saying my vows. I really didn't think much about it at the time; however, I knew without a doubt that a higher being was present. A glimpse from the Lord, and yet no acknowledgement from me.

Before I knew it, one month into our marriage, I became pregnant with our first daughter. To be newlyweds and pregnant was a very exciting time, and yet we were just beginning to learn about each other. I was trying to get the hang of being a wife, managing the awful smells around me, and planning for a little girl to join us soon. Quite emotional times for me, but also quite a joyful time.

When our daughter was nine months old, I became pregnant with our second daughter. Pregnancy went amazingly smooth that is until I was placed on bed rest. She was born healthy at thirty-seven weeks. In the sleep-deprived weeks to come, I would become overwhelmed with trying to take care of two little girls eighteen months apart.

Full time employee, wife, and mother to two little girls began to take a toll on me to say the least. I started to feel like my life was unraveling out of control rather quickly.

I was left feeling like someone had punctured the air in my tires. I had everything—a great husband, a great job, two beautiful little girls, yet somehow, I was lost… why? I remember waking extremely early one morning and couldn't sleep. I picked up the Bible, which I had not even thought about in years and started reading, and not just a passage, but several for hours after hours. I was certain I believed in God; however, I had never exactly committed myself. I decided I was going to get back into going to church. For several weeks, I tried a few different churches and then decided on one that was just down the street from our home.

# Going Back to Church

I would bring my two little girls with me to church on Sundays encouraging my oldest to attend Sunday school. We came for months and enjoyed it. I was always hopeful my little one would be quiet or sleep, so I could listen to the pastor's sermon. Sometimes, I was able to even relax and enjoy myself in church; however, other times, it felt overwhelming trying to calm a crying baby in church.

I began a new job of employment and began to recognize some familiar faces I had seen in church. I remember one of the ladies I worked with and attended church with one day ask me, "Do you know if you are going to heaven?" Wow I had never been so intimidated by a question in my entire existence! I took what seemed like forever to respond to her question. I thought about it and said, "Yes, I think so, I think I'm a good person." It wouldn't be until many years later that I would be able to really answer that question with no reservations.

# Praying for What's to Come

I was getting the grasp of trying to incorporate church and religion into my life of work, marriage, and children. I began to pray to God for a son. Approximately one year prior to conceiving our son, Noah, I had prayed and asked God several times for a little boy. After two girls, I was hopeful and felt destined to conceive a son. I remember one day while driving hearing on the radio a woman's call into a Christian talk show reporting she had prayed for her son, and God had blessed her with a little boy whom later would be diagnosed with a disability. Why that resonated with me at that time I had no idea. Little did I know, God was making a way and preparing me for the little boy he would very soon bless me with.

My third pregnancy. I can't quite explain it; however, I knew as soon as the pregnancy test was positive that God had granted me my request to have a son. I had never felt quite the conviction at this point in my life as I did that day. I knew I was carrying a little boy inside of me. I remember the excitement of knowing my prayers had been answered!

My husband was so worried I would be disappointed during the ultrasound to find out we were pregnant with yet another girl. He even went so far as to tell me, "Sorry, honey, I really feel like we are meant to have all girls." Now, don't get me wrong, I have three girls whom I love dearly and wouldn't change for anything. I continued to have strong feelings I was carrying a son. I remember feeling like it was my secret because I was the only one with all my heart that believed a little boy to be growing within me. My third pregnancy was full of nausea as well as karate kicks. I remember losing many nights of sleep and feeling exhausted by the end of the day because of this little one inside of me. He truly was a rock star in the womb, a one-man band whom I knew was an answered prayer.

# The Day of the Ultrasound

I had never invited my mother to an ultrasound appointment prior, but I knew how excited she would be to find out I was carrying her first grandson. I even had a little wager going with my husband about the gender of the baby determining who decided on where we ate lunch following the appointment.

The ultrasound monitor was no more than turned on and the technician asked if we would like to know the gender of the baby, as the baby was ready to show us! The sweet words of victory. "You are having a boy!" I remember feeling overcome with emotion as tears clouded my eyes. Thank you, God, for answering my prayers!

I'm sure there wasn't a dry eye in the exam room at that moment. My mom couldn't wait to call my dad to inform him of their new grandchild, a grandson.

We were overcome with happiness, and I had a sense of peace knowing God had been listening to me all those months when I had been praying consistently for a son. Why then did I not give him all the glory that he was owed, surely it was his doing and not mine.

# Choosing a Name

My husband and I tossed and turned on little boy names. I had always liked the name, Maverick James; however, now that I was pregnant with a little boy, I just wasn't so sure about that name anymore. I remember watching movie films and continuing to see and hear the name, Noah. Finally, one day, I asked my husband what he thought of the name, Noah. He liked the name, Noah, and we decided we would give our two little girls the choice of names we were contemplating. The girls, when asked if they preferred the name, Maverick or Noah, didn't hesitate to reply rather quickly with the name, Noah, or as they would say Moah! Our little boy's name was settled, we would call him Noah Ray. Noah's middle name is named after his great grandfather. I am so happy we chose to name him, Noah Ray. His great grandfather was overjoyed to hear we had named our son in honor of him.

The Hebrew name Noah means "rest and repose". According to the old testament, Noah was the builder of the Ark that allowed him, his family, and animals of each species to survive the great flood. (behindthename.com)

# Feeling Uneasy

As the months passed, I began to have feelings of uneasiness. Doctor's appointments went great, and our little boy was growing as expected. I remember one day confiding in my mom about my uneasy feelings. I felt like something was wrong with my unborn son. I had absolutely no idea what was wrong or how serious, but I was very adamant something wasn't quite right. I tried to chalk it up to jitters as this was my first son whom I had prayed many prayers for. Maybe I was just scared because I was receiving the little boy I had always dreamed of.

I tried to shake this insane feeling that something was wrong with my little boy, but still it remained and continued to reside in me. I had an overwhelming sense of needing to protect this little boy with no real reason to feel such things. To this day, I continue to have this feeling. I know it is the Lord who has put those feelings within me, as much as I'd like to say its mother's intuition, it's the Lord's work. The Lord was preparing me to love and care for our special little boy.

# Delivery day

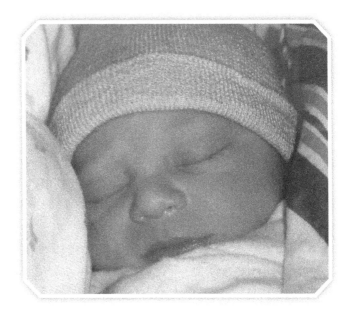

Our beautiful eight-pound baby boy, Noah, was born March 8, 2012. Noah was delivered quite easily and peacefully. I remember feeling content watching the nurses attending to my newborn son while the doctor continued to work on me. I don't remember too much in the craziness of those moments to follow the birth of our son. The room became flooded with emergency staff shortly after Noah's birth. At one point, I remember not feeling like I was quite with it. I was not at all able to focus on anything other than my doctor who assured me I was going to be fine. I remember trusting the doctor and closing my eyes feeling complete peace and comfort wash over me.

Unsure of how long I was in this state, I remember opening my eyes to see my husband, son, and doctor in the delivery room. I was reassured I was going to be okay. I had begun to hemorrhage following the birth of our son. During pregnancy, we were unaware of the placenta attaching, as almost growing into the wall of my uterus. I am thankful for my wonderful doctor and the Lord for giving him the knowledge and hands to work his miracle on me that day.

Feelings of exhaustion flooded me, I remember requiring assistance to hold my son and to nurse him. I was unable to get up out of bed for a day and required total assistance with our newborn son. He was so beautiful and perfect. Words cannot describe how much of an amazing moment it was to introduce the two girls to their baby brother, "baby moah." We were overjoyed to leave the hospital a few days later all healthy with our bundle of joy! Praise God! I am not sure I ever gave God the glory he truly deserved that day. My son was alive and healthy, everything felt right in the world at that moment.

# Life continues

It's amazing how God has continuously showed up in my life and not given up on me even though I have never given him the glory he has more than deserved. Looking back, I see that my prayers have been selfish, all for me and my desires. Such amazing miracles performed in my life and still I never asked for Jesus to come into my life. I had heard about Jesus, I had even stood in church asking for forgiveness, yet somehow always falling short. I continued to go to church; however, with three children, things once again became hectic, and I let myself fall victim to excuses once again.

My son was growing and was healthy, he was going for blood work once a week to check on his jaundice, which was clearing up well. Still that uneasy feeling resided within me.

One morning, I was taking my son out of his car seat and watched before my eyes as he became red like a lobster! I was beyond hysterical, and my mom, who was also with me, saw what was happening. We called the doctors immediately and took him to see the pediatrician. Behind my son's left arm was a small inflamed looking circular reddish in color marking.

Long story short, we went to several doctors' appointments with several different doctors with several different theories and several different potent antibiotics to try… none of which were the answer. In fact, the ointments and Band-Aids on his skin seemed to make things worse. Noah began to form little pustular bubbles on his skin filled with fluid. The dreaded feelings I had been having since before I had given birth to him were very much on my mind at this point. Was this what was being foretold to me that would be wrong with my son? What in the world is wrong with Noah? Is he going to be okay?

One of the diagnoses that were being thrown around at the time was MRSA…of course with me working in the health care field, my first thought was I had somehow brought it home from work to my poor little boy. I was beyond frightened and thought this had been what God must have been preparing me for. I remember going into church that Sunday after hearing MRSA with tears in my eyes asking my pastor at the time to please pray for my son that he would be healed. Finally, after several agonizing weeks, I decided to take my son for yet another opinion since the next step was sounding like draining the pustule which meant cutting into my little boys' arm! My son was referred to a dermatologist within days with a diagnosis of mastocytoma (a type of mastocytosis that presents as a solitary collection of mast cells in the skin. Mast cells are made in the bone marrow and are part of the body's immune system).

These cells, once activated, release a variety of proteins and chemicals that create allergic reactions and attract other cell types to fight off infections (AOCD). Relief, music to a mother's ears, my little boy is going to be okay! My son continues to have this mastocytoma behind his left arm to this day. If the mastocytoma is rubbed just right, it will flare up, and he will flush red; however, symptoms have lessened as he has grown.

Noah continued to grow within the next year meeting his milestones, beginning to talk, walk, and run through the house like the sweet little boy I had always dreamt of. Now when I say talk, I mean one word like, "mama," "dada," or "no." He was holding my gaze and smiling and was quite the happy camper. He even enjoyed having his picture taken. He loved his two older sisters who carried him around the house and pampered him. I began to settle down and become content thinking I must have been crazy to think up these feelings that something could possibly be wrong with this sweet little boy of mine.

Noah was and is one of my most loving and sensitive kids. Noah has always enjoyed being rocked and cuddled from the time he was born. My son has always been extremely tender and close to me. From the time I brought him home until present day, he has always come to me for his daily needs. He loves his daddy very much as well but has always came to me for his needs. There is something to be said about a mother's role in a child's life. Children seem to know that their mothers are there to nurture them and contend to their needs. A father is also a necessity and every much as vital a role in a child's life. I just know from my own personal experience that my children tend to come to me for everything. My kids always come to me for food inquiries, even if my husband is standing in the kitchen right next to the refrigerator!

# Terrible Twos, Threes, and Fours

Who turned the lights out? Noah was no longer the little boy I remembered who used to look up at me, instead this little boy turned his eyes from me and no longer wanted to hold my gaze. Many times, I called to you by your name, but you did not answer. I would not hear from my sweet little boy again until just before his fifth birthday. I have several photos from when Noah was a baby where he was hamming it up with his cute little grin with eyes that stared into the camera. Where did those beautiful eyes go? And why did you no longer smile at the very family that loves you unconditionally.

These were some of the darkest days, months and longest years of my life. My son no longer could talk to me. He preferred to watch movies and sometimes watch them until we had to peel his fingers from the remote control. He demanded total control of his world around him. Noah still liked to be held, but everything had become on his terms alone. He began having major blow-ups and tantrums that lasted far longer than I had ever imagined possible. When looking into his eyes during these awful meltdowns, it was like looking into glossy glazed over empty eyes. I'm not even sure he was reachable at those moments. What was causing these terrible outbursts? These bouts of frenzy Noah would have could last anywhere from five minutes or up to a half an hour at times.

I remember the awful screams and uncontrollable flailing around of his limbs as he threw himself on the floor and furniture. I remember trying to remove any toys or items that may harm him from his destructive path. I felt helpless as I tried to gain control of the uncontrollable situation. I could not reach him, he could not hear me, and I was unable to comfort him. I sat helpless watching him through these awful moments that became a frequent way of behavior for quite some time. What in the world had happened to my loving little boy? I wanted my sweet baby boy back. Who was this new little boy replacing my Noah? It was like riding this enormous out of control wave never knowing which direction it was turning or what would be destroyed in its path. I felt utterly hopeless with no idea of how to calm Noah.

I missed my sweet little boy whom felt like had been so unfairly taken from me. I can't quite put into words the feelings of loss I felt during this time. A part of me was mourning the loss of the little boy I remembered. I was trying to accommodate what felt like a much different little boy that was taking on this role of my son. Unfortunately, things would get much worse before better. Noah began tearing at his face, arms, and legs unable to listen or hear the word, "stop," coming from my mouth. I remember blood streaming down his face mixing with angry tears not having any reasons to give for such awful behaviors. I felt like a total failure.

Where did I fail as a parent? What did I do to ever deserve this? I began to blame myself and question myself as a parent. I became consumed, to say the least, with what I could have possibly done to cause these changes in my little boy. I was in a dark place with even darker circles under my eyes for the enormous amount of stress that was consuming me. I was nothing short of a complete mess.

I felt alone and completely lost. I was trying to keep things together for my three children and husband, but I was lost. I was hopeless, heartbroken, and quite angry. Thank God for my husband, mother, and two little girls for loving me in the midst of my nightmare. I spent hours, which turned into days, going through everything I had done or could have possibly done while pregnant or while nursing that could have somehow caused me to hurt my little boy. I remember occasionally talking about my fears to my husband and mother; however, I mostly kept my fears to myself. I can't quite put into words the sense of loneliness or desperation that resided within my heart. I was beyond awkward and felt separated from the world. Even though I had family to turn to that saw what I was going through who were also going through the same thing, I was oblivious to the other passengers around me. Encouraging words went in one ear and out the other. I was beyond reach to others at this time. I remember holding my son and crying with such exhaustion, and somehow Noah's exhaustion did not come. Who had unleashed this nightmare upon me, and how could I continue to deal with this day in and day out?

My husband and I no longer went out with friends or went out together very often unless our parents watched our kids. My husband and I felt rather trapped at home with Noah's unpredictable behaviors. And no one seemed to be able to relate or really understand what we were going through. We were not a normal family, or at least we no longer felt like a normal family. My husband and I had to strategically plan to get any type of time together. My husband and I were exhausted. We no longer did things as a family. I would get out for a while, come home, and my husband would take off. It was a very trying time for our family.

We were literally just trying to survive during these times. We felt as if we were taking shifts with kiddy patrol. My daughters also felt the stress and strain of Noah's behavior. I felt enormous guilt for the challenges our family was facing. I am very grateful for my husband's patience and continued love especially during this whirl wind of emotions I was going through. I was not a very easy person to get along with during these times, and I often shut down with quite a short fuse. My two daughters didn't understand why Noah was lashing out at all of us. I had no answers for their questions.

I apologized to my daughters frequently for my son's bad behaviors. On more than one occasion, my son had lashed out on my other children, physically hurting them and scaring them at times. If they were playing with a toy he wanted, he would literally fight them for it. I could not leave my son alone in a room with my other children for fear that he may harm them. Noah had freakish strength and was hard at times for me to manage. Many times, I received blows from Noah's angry fists and feet. Car rides quickly turned to destructive rides. Noah could not handle more than fifteen to thirty minutes in the car and would start picking his skin or his face, arms, and legs until they bled. Within minutes, his body would be covered in blood before I could pull the car over in time to stop the damage.

Years back in college, I had gotten the chance to work with several different children with different diagnosis. I couldn't shake the feeling that my son's behavior was not the so called "normal" behavior for children. Little boys will be little boys, and since I had only ever known little girls, I was told many times boys develop differently. So, for a while., I tried to roll with the new ways of this little boy Noah, my son whom seemed so very distant these days. I began asking Noah's doctor about his delays and abnormal behavioral outbursts.

I asked the doctor about trying speech therapy services in hopes of bringing back Noah's voice. In the thirty minutes we were there, he latched onto me for the first twenty minutes and then finally the last ten minutes would play with the therapist. He did begin to attempt play with the therapists, but with no real success. We were not getting very far in our journey with therapy after several weeks, and our insurance visits had since dried up. We were then referred to Help Me Grow home services. My son began showing interest in the new toys Help Me Grow would bring, and he did learn a bit of sign language to help with communication. Mainly simple sign language for instance: eat, more, and drink. These signs of communication were a tremendous help at this point, and it was exciting to see

Noah make an effort to initiate a form of communication with us.

When Noah turned three, he was eligible to attend pre-school at the local city school, which just so happened to have an amazing class specific to his needs. Our family and son would become blessed with a teacher and friend that would for years be what we referred to as our saving grace! We have been so very blessed to receive guidance and assistance from Noah's amazing teacher that didn't have to go above and beyond for him but did! My son took to his teacher and began signing with her, listening, and behaviors were getting slightly better and even dare I say somewhat manageable. I was learning how to steer the storm or at least get his attention on other things that he found enjoyment in. We were finally able to engage our son in the simple act of play.

We began to see Noah smile and show signs of enjoying himself, which we hadn't seen in a very long time. Noah began receiving occupational therapy and speech therapy services at school as well as trained specialized teachers to accommodate his needs. Noah began responding to the school's interventions, and things were slowly going in an upward direction. I cannot even begin to explain how amazingly kind and helpful all of the staff that worked with my son and continue to work with my son are. They have laughed with my son, cried with my son, and I'm pretty sure had some pretty rough days with my son.

To this present day, my son continues to have a wonderful relationship with his very first teacher. She continues to play a vital role in his life and continued development. I am often notified from Noah when too much time has passed, and he has not been to see her. She has been such a breath of fresh air for our family and has given us hope more than she will ever know. Those of you who have a son or daughter with a disability can understand how difficult and hard it is to trust others with the care of our special little ones. It has been wonderful to have another adult who understands and whom I can completely trust with my little man.

With my background in occupational therapy, I began to encourage learning through play. Often, on afternoons following school, I would try to encourage Noah to further sign language or use of learning cards. I would verbally give him the word of an object or animal on one of the cards and ask him to retrieve it from a pile I had set out on the floor around him. We were learning that Noah understood exactly what we were asking of him. Noah was able to go on to learn the names of animals, colors, numbers, and letters. Noah was showing us he was able to retain information and capable of learning new information. I was so excited to see Noah taking steps to engage himself in learning. For a great while, Noah allowed me to work with him; however, it became very clear to me by my son that my role was his mother, not his teacher. Noah was in so many words without saying any words telling me to stick to my role as his mother—maybe after a day of school and then me trying to push more on him became too much, I'm not sure.

Noah began getting frustrated with me when I would try to work with him to the point of behaviors. I decided to give it a break for a while. I understand now that Noah liked knowing I was there after school, not to necessarily push him further with his learning, but to just enjoy spending time with him. For a long time after I would pick him up from school, he would just like to rock in the recliner with me and watch cartoons. Noah was letting me know what he wanted and what worked for him, which was wonderful and so helpful compared to what we had previously been dealing with.

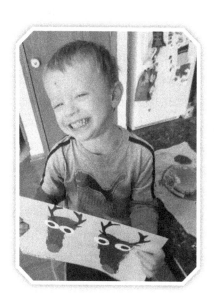

# Another Baby

I became pregnant with my fourth child during this time. I was beyond frightened to be adding yet another child into the mix of what was already what seemed beyond stressful. I'm not going to sugar coat it, it was tough dealing with pregnancy while also dealing with Noah's demanding ways and behaviors. I was so scared of how he would treat the baby and how he would share me with this new baby.

After my third daughter was born, I was pleasantly surprised how well Noah behaved around her. He was very sweet, kind, and even sometimes helpful retrieving items for me when I was busy with the baby. It took me six months to feel confident enough to let Noah hold his baby sister. Some of the most loving moments I will cherish are of Noah and his sister looking at each other while sitting in Noah's lap together. He truly loves his sister. Watching the two of them grow together has been a wonderful gift. I had days where I would cry because my little girl was starting to talk, and here my son, who was three years older, still was unable to communicate words to me. It didn't seem quite fair to see Noah struggling so much while his baby sister was cruising through her milestones. I have a recording to this day on my phone of a video of a time when I was in the car, and they both began trying to talk to one another.

Noah's voice sounded so high pitched it is extremely hard to make out what he is trying to say. It was very hard to see him struggle to talk while his baby sister was beginning to talk with no reservations. Noah was always very kind and gentle with his baby sister. Actually, she is the one, and still is to this day that is my more outgoing and the shenanigan starter if you will. She loves to stir things up in the house. From an early age, my youngest wanted to be a part of everything, she was very adamant from a young age that she was the "boss baby."

This little girl was beginning to attempt to run the show in the house. And for the most part, it worked! My son learned to share me quite well, and I made quite the effort to always make sure he didn't feel left out in anyway. My son would start going to his father for more assistance, which was wonderful and freed me up quite a bit as well. This gave him time to build a relationship with someone other than myself. Noah was getting closer to his dad and letting more people get close to him.

After several years and visiting specialists, Noah was officially diagnosed with non-verbal autism and ADHD in 2016. For a long while, we had assumed he had autism; however, the actual diagnosis was a whole other issue of obtaining. Many specialists continued to see him but not feel sure about exactly what his differences were to be called. I kept hearing how crucial early intervention was; however, how was I supposed to obtain early intervention without a diagnosis?

I am very fortunate to know someone who had previously been through this very journey with her own son and was able to lead me in the right direction. Noah began using an iPad as his voice to increase his ease with communication. He did amazing and began communicating his needs to us, finally in a way we were able to understand! Now, don't get me wrong, things were no piece of cake, but we were finally making headway with our son's journey with autism.

As I write this, it's amazing to think of how far he has come in such a short time. How did I never thank God during this wild yet beautiful storm? Noah was showing us a glimpse into his world where he was very much the little boy I remembered. He was able to ask us for things and very simply say hello or goodnight just as our other children. He enjoyed his iPad so much, which we came to call his talker. What an amazing blessing to have, a form of communication to conversate with the world around him. For quite a few months, Noah continued to use his talker as well as sign language or grabbing my hand to lead me to his desires.

He became quite silly while using his talker and even laughed over crazy conversation and pictures presented on his communication program. One of the biggest communication issues for Noah was always food, he wanted to be able to express his desire to eat out or shall I say get fast food! From quite an early age Noah, began showing interest in McDonalds, Wendy's, and Burger King. I remember at one time putting pictures of restaurants in my photo album on my phone so I could easily access them for his communication needs. Noah has always had an opinion and has always been more than willing to express it, just not always able to communicate it effectively.

Wherever Noah went, his talker went. The talker became as much a part of Noah as his other daily attire. He would take pictures of his friends, teachers, and family with voice programming for easy access for communicating with them. There was no doubt about it, things were looking up for Noah. He was having fewer frustrating moments. Teachers began to notice and comment how Noah was becoming much more eager to learn and listen to instructions provided during class time.

Noah was smiling with a little pep in his step, even displaying some socialization skills with other children his age. What a concept—sharing, taking turns, and following directions. Noah was not exactly close to mastering these concepts; however, he was making major progress! His siblings were attempting to include him in games and pretend play. I remember one weekend I was feeling super ambitious and decided to take Noah to a sensory movie playing at the local theatre in town. Noah, being overwhelmed, was beyond an understatement! There were so many children present in the theatre with so many different reactions that Noah just couldn't handle it. He was unable to sit still through the movie showing a wide variety of emotions, needless to say, we did not make it for the entire movie, and we left.

I was beyond overwhelmed, upset doesn't begin to explain how I felt. Looking back now, I'm pretty sure the noise of the other children along with the movie was just too much input for Noah to sort through. The problem was, his siblings did not want to leave the theatre. The other kids were enjoying themselves and enjoying their day out watching a new movie. How does one tell their family we must leave because your brother can't handle being at the movies? "Unfair" is a word I have become very accustomed to hearing.

# Life Isn't Fair

Why is our brother so different? Why can't Noah talk like everyone else? Why are we catering to Noah? Why can we not do more things outside of the house? Why does Noah always get his way…and the list goes on and on and on. To this day, I frequently hear these words. My older children sometimes understand, but a little part of them always just seems to feel a bit shorted. My husband and I have had many conversations regarding Noah's special needs and his difficulty understanding responsibilities. This does not make it any easier for children to understand why their immediate lives must be so different from their friends and other families.

My daughters were somewhat embarrassed to have their friends over, or shall I say worried because they never knew how Noah may behave. Kids have an automatic response to see kids and want to be around other kids. This posed a problem, as my girls did not exactly want their brother hanging out with them while they were entertaining guests. Which, hello, doesn't every little brother want to tag along with their older siblings?! *Yes*, the problem was the poor girls never knew what to expect whether it be Noah wanting to just tag along or hug them, or throw toys, it really was anyone's guess on how Noah's behavior would swing that day.

I remember shipping Noah off to his grandparents one day so that my oldest daughter could enjoy her birthday without any interruptions from her brother. This only led me to feel guilty, how could I send one of my children away just so that my other children could feel *normal!* Was I getting this parenting thing all wrong? How do I incorporate my other children's feelings and not hurt our family as a whole?

The answer, well, there is no answer to that one, at least not for me. I will never make all my children immediately happy with the decisions I make for our family when it comes to dealing with our outside of the box family.

# Miracle in the Midst of the Storm

2017

A little before Noah's fifth birthday, I was given news that I would be needing surgery. As the weeks approached, I was nervous how my kids would handle Mom not being available to help with their daily needs. I was especially nervous about Noah. He has always relied on me for so much. I have become his go to person over the years. I didn't want Noah to think I was avoiding him, as Noah has always been a very emotional little boy whose feelings can be easily offended. I wasn't sure Noah would understand that mommy required time to heal and recuperate from surgery.

I hugged and kissed my children goodbye and promised them I would be seeing them very soon. I explained that they need not worry, as I would soon be back to myself.

My kids were so excited to come back home after their short stay with their grandparents during this time. I remember the kids coming through the door, not sure of how close they should get to me or if it was safe to touch me. I reassured them that I was okay, that they needed to be sure no one jumped into my lap until my ouchies were healed. The kids came with hugs and kisses content to know I was home and well.

Noah sat beside me and began to ever so gently pet my arm as if I were the most fragile porcelain doll that could break at any moment. His face was so sincere and loving, I couldn't help but to hold back tears as I ruffled his hair. I remember looking into his eyes and seeing his eyes actually looking back at me. What an absolutely amazing moment. "I love you, Noah," I said, and behold, Noah said, "I love you too, Mama." (absolute ugly tears stain my face as I am typing this, I can barely make out the keys and screen. I still get chills thinking back to this magical moment)

*My son can talk!* My son has found his voice! Thank you, God, you are so good! Yes, I acknowledge it is by the grace of God that my son has found his voice! I do believe in my heart that the Lord is responsible for this miraculous miracle! What a light of hope for our family and supporters who have worked so hard with our little guy. One of the most beautiful moments of my life, a moment I will cherish as long as I am breathing. I have literally witnessed God's work first hand through my little boy, not once, but time and time again.

During the months and next year, Noah begins to go on to speak sentences and hold conversations. Noah still continues with speech therapy services and occupational therapy as well as specialized classes to meet his needs. He grows by leaps and bounds that I hate to almost admit I never quite let myself believe could be possible. My son is literally beating the odds, fighting this battle they call non-verbal autism. I am beyond humbled and grateful. Words cannot express the feelings of joy and happiness my husband and I felt that day.

The days to follow would bring a flood of words. Noah had a vocabulary! He was talking saying several words. Words that can only be described as music to a mother's ears, this mothers ears! Noah continues to broaden his vocabulary, words turn into sentences, and Noah is able to hold a conversation with his teachers and family. By God's grace, Noah has found his voice! What an amazing journey we had been on for the last several years leading to this amazing point where Noah finds his voice. Boy did he find his voice! He became quite the chatterbox, and how amazing indeed to hear that sweet little voice!

Noah has always been rather hyper and has difficulty with his attention to task. Noah prefers to have things done for him and requires encouragement for attempting tasks on his own. Noah asked me one morning while I was getting him ready for school if I would quit my job so I could take care of him. Heartbreak doesn't begin to explain how I felt when he asked me that question. My son expects me to take care of all of his needs...*all!* Noah can be downright demanding of me at times insisting on me being the parent to take on all of his needs. My husband is wonderful with him and offers his help; however, Noah gives him a hard time and insists on me. We as parents have tried to divide up Noah's demands in a routine of sorts in order for Noah to be forced into getting used to both of us taking care of him. Noah continues daily to fight for me to take him to bed and pick him up from school, both of which are my husband's tasks.

I have taken on the early hours of the day for getting Noah up and ready for school in the mornings. After more than a year of this routine my son still asks me literally everyday if I will complete "ALL" of these tasks for him. He is a persistent little fella that's for sure! Once in a great while, I will have the day off of work or get off of work early and surprise him. It truly is awesome to see that happy surprised smile he gives me when I do these little things for him. Noah shows appreciation and remorse, sometimes within the same hour. He actually is a very grateful little boy who remembers the little things.

He constantly reminds me of the little things and how important the little things in life are. At school, Noah is continuing to make huge gains, breaking down barriers we never knew he would be able to reach let alone conquer. Noah begins to use his talker less and less at this point since he is talking so efficiently. He still continues to keep his talker within arm's reach, maybe out of comfort, or maybe because he likes the independence of having information at his fingertips. I do believe Noah's iPad has taught him how to be more independent with his learning. Noah has learned how to navigate through the internet quite well for his needs.

I have had a few in depth talks with Noah about what he remembers before he was able to speak. Of course as in depth as a child his age is capable of. Noah has been able to verbally express how angry and sad he felt when he was unable to talk or relay his wants and needs to us. Noah further went on to tell me that the music from the radio in the car bothered him. For a long time, I would ask Noah if he preferred the radio on or off while in the car. After school, Noah did not like extra noise, in fact he did not even like me asking too many questions about his day. I have learned that by the time my husband or I picked him up from school, he has pretty much checked out and just wants quiet time to himself. When Noah returns home from school, he likes to sit in a quiet place with just his talker. He is obsessed like every other kid, watching videos and short clips on YouTube. He does not sit on his talker all night, so I allow this time for him to unwind. I've learned to only ask him, "What was your favorite thing you did today at school?" in order to show him I am still interested in his day but not prying either.

Over the years, Noah has become more forthcoming on aspects of his school day. This information is brought forth by him, as he decides what he likes to share with us. We are thankful for wonderful teachers that communicate how our son is doing in school since he isn't always forth coming on this information.

Noah is drawn to the water and finds so much enjoyment playing in the water. We live close to open water, and I have always been so nervous with Noah's fascination with water. We enrolled Noah in an adaptive swim lesson at our local rec center. What a great enjoyment swimming has become for our son. Not only is he gaining confidence and learning swimming skills, but he is becoming knowledgeable and safe around water.

He continues to receive swim lessons through the years from a wonderfully patient and kind swim instructor who just so happens to be an occupational therapist. Noah continues to enjoy swimming and taking lessons. It has been such a joy to watch Noah learn how to swim and find his own enjoyment with an extracurricular activity. I remember one of Noah's first swim lessons mainly being the ability to handle pouring or rather sprinkling water over his head, neck, and shoulders. Noah has come so far with his swim lessons. Noah continues to be quite fearless of the water; however, he displays much more safety and skill than I ever thought or knew possible.

We are adjusting to our little boy's voice, and the increase ease of life around us as things become a tad bit easier and somewhat comfortable. My husband and I are over joyed at our son's progress. It has been such an amazing sight to see Noah transforming. Noah and his dad have become the best of buddies and are sharing moments together building Legos and forts creating an amazing bond. Noah is ready to move on to kindergarten, what a scary thought for me as a mother! New teachers to adjust to when I loved my son's teachers and trusted them completely. I felt somewhat vulnerable and nervous at how Noah would do with a classroom full of "regular" children.

# Rock Star

This is the name my son's teachers have given my son over the years. I remember one of the first times hearing my son being called a rock star and me thinking, *Huh, are we talking about the same child?* And you know what, my son is totally a rock star! Noah has come such a long way, he has put in a lot of hard work. As I sat at a table surrounded by my son's teacher's, I found myself feeling quite presently surprised to say the least. The teachers informed me that my son was receiving passing grades and was no longer in need of occupational therapy services at the time. He would probably not be needing to continue being pulled from the class for much longer because they felt this may actually be hindering him. I believe with all my heart that the Lord has at precisely the right times placed certain people within Noah's life to teach him certain skills. Noah's instructors have amazing patience, kindness, and drive necessary and responsible for his success. Perfect timing, God's timing is utterly perfect.

Noah is my constant reminder of patience, love, and kindness. Hey, isn't that what the very word of the Lord teaches us? Coincidence? I think not! Could it be the very child that is teaching me all of these things could possibly be teaching me a much bigger lesson?

In awe as we are of our jabbering little man, we eventually continued with our life. Noah is communicating wonderfully, still has some behavioral issues, and is still learning there is no *I* in team. Noah tends to march to the beat of his own drum, he is quirky, and quite funky to say the least. Our son is extremely loving and kind; however, these emotions can easily be turned to anger and sorrow. My son expresses all emotions instantly, there is no filter. I will always know where I stand with Noah. He is never afraid to inform me of when he is unhappy with a decision of mine. Noah can also be extremely loving and kind. I have watched him give many sweet compliments and gestures to his sisters and myself out of the pure sweetness of his heart.

One minute, Noah can be smiling, and the next minute, he can be hollering and crying. It can at times seem like quite a rollercoaster of emotions coming from him. He is not always able to be rational, in these moments, I try my hardest to remain calm and talk very softly within reason to his overacting self. I've learned over the years that yelling at my son only upsets and hurts the both of us more. Now, don't get me wrong, I am far from perfect and fall victim to yelling at times. I do know that if I get down to my son's level and stay calm and gentle with him, he is able to calm the storm within and focus on me for a moment to control his emotions.

I am learning to emotionally connect with Noah, which has been quite difficult at times. I have learned to keep things simple with Noah with simple directions with fewer steps that are easier for him to understand and perform. My expectations are not the same as my son's; however, Noah is a procrastinator and does not like to be rushed in anyway. I have to be very direct and persistent with him. If I give an inch, my son will most eminently take a mile.

# Mornings

Mornings are so very challenging in our household. I have four children to get ready and out the door by 6:00 a.m. It's exhausting to say in the least. I very rarely get out the door by 6:00AM its more like a quarter after with hopes of actually leaving on time. I get up very early in the morning to give myself time to get ready. Including a very strong cup of coffee before I head upstairs to wake up the rest of the crew. Needless to say, my children are not morning people. Noah hates to be rushed around and tends to tune me out; therefore, requiring a ton of patience on my part. Which, in turn, usually stresses me out putting me in a rather grouchy state myself.

Several times, I have to tell Noah to get dressed, eat, and come to the counter, so I can give him his medicine and brush his teeth. My least favorite part of the day to say the least. I have left for work many times in tears of defeat. All four of my children somehow seem to gang up on me at my most vulnerable moment, the early morning hours. I have speed dialed my husband's phone number many times with my frustrations of my early morning tyrraids with the kids. I especially remember one morning feeling totally defeated begging my husband to please switch me shifts, which would mean him taking the morning shift leaving me to pick up the kids in the afternoon. My kids are always happy when done with school for the day, imagine that!

One awful morning in particular, I remember feeling beyond defeated but rather hopeless in my situation with the kids. The four kids were beyond awful on this morning, and I honestly just couldn't bare thinking of just one more day of this absolute craziness. My kids were struggling to get their butts moving and required far too many cues from me necessary for completing their morning routines. It felt like the first day of school, except without the enthusiasm; however, was the same routine performed consistently on a day to day basis. I was ready to pull my hair out from the roots and throw a tantrum myself! How had this become my life? I never dreamed the very kids I love could make me feel this crazy and out of control. This particular morning, I felt as if all four of my children had decided to either argue or go on strike from getting ready for school. When did my kids gain control over me? How did I create an Army that works against me instead of with me? My entire day felt ruined and I was beyond drained. I was yelling at the walls for all I could tell. Who had I become; surely this is not the parent I had anticipated becoming.

My entire day felt ruined because of the rough morning I had just experienced. Tears of anger, frustration, hurt, and defeat stung my eyes all the way to work on my long commute. I could not shake the events of the morning. I hate to admit it, but I wasn't looking forward to seeing them that afternoon, and I wasn't quite sure how I could handle another morning like I had just went through. The afternoon proved to be not much better either. As soon as

I returned home, the demands began. I was still grouchy from the morning, tired from work, and the last thing I wanted to do was to put up with the kids and their shenanigans over dinner. My kids sometimes forget that I am not a restaurant at dinner and tend to blurt out their interests in something different. "Mom do this, mom do that", my patience was wearing extremely thin. I could not take just one more demand!

Finally, I decided I had had enough. I was going to turn into bed early with hopes of forgetting the previous events of the day before they all began all too early the next morning. I told my husband and children good night, went upstairs, and prepared for sleep. Instead, tears of desperation spilled down my cheeks. I felt hopeless, I was being pulled in so many different directions. Everyone seemed to want a piece of me, and there was just not enough of me to go around. I felt like such a failure to my children, my husband, and myself. I didn't even recognize myself anymore. I felt like all I ever did was yell at my children's poor behavior.

I was spiraling out of control, drowning with no sign of a life raft within my reach. *Jesus, I cried, I can't do this anymore, please help me*, I pleaded! I couldn't manage four kids, working full time, being a wife, keeping house, and etc. I then began apologizing for everything throughout my life, things I hadn't thought about in years. Sins I had never accounted for were finally being brought to light.

I woke feeling like I had never really slept, that something supernatural had happened throughout the night, like I had somehow been up apologizing for my entire life while also sleeping at the same time. How is that even possible? What in the world was going on? I don't know, but somehow, I felt an odd sense of hope and an overwhelming desire to get to work to be baptized. What in the world...I know it sounds quite odd, so let me back track just a bit to months prior.

# The Believer

As I explained earlier, I am an occupational therapy assistant. I work in a nursing facility providing skilled therapy services. I had the privilege and honor of working with an amazing man, a very godly man. I will refer to him as *the believer* throughout my story. He, the believer, began preaching the word during our treatments together. I'm pretty sure I received more out of our sessions than I could have possibly ever given him. He began giving me a glimpse into the word, explaining scripture, giving me hope, making me think beyond earthly things. I remember one day the believer and I were having a discussion revolving around abortion…I know, sticky subject!

I remember stating that I personally could never have an abortion because I believed in the right to life. He then began to tell me a story, a story about people holding bibles while standing near an abortion clinic screaming about freedom of life as women entered and exited the building. The believer then proceeded to ask me what Jesus would have done. I didn't quite know what to think or how to answer his question.

The believer spoke of Jesus comforting the broken hearted and being a place to lay burdens, to rely solely on him to find comfort and rest. He then proceeded to tell me through tears how Jesus would have comforted these women and shown love and kindness, all the while pointing them on the path to righteousness. At that moment, I felt like I had just a glimpse or a small taste of the love Jesus has for us. For months, the believer taught my coworkers and myself many lessons from the Bible. The believer was bringing my coworkers and I closer together with his teachings, we were eager to hear his stories and many lessons he was so willing to share. After many months of being ministered to by my patient, the believer mentioned to me one day, "When you are ready to be baptized, let me know." I am almost ashamed to admit I really hadn't thought twice about it since I had been baptized Catholic as a child. So, I tucked that little invitation for baptism away.

> Ask and it will be given to you; seek and
> you will find; knock and the door will be
> opened to you. For everyone who asks
> receives; the one who seeks finds; and the
> one who knocks, the door will be opened.
> (Matt. 7–8, NIV)

I stepped out of my car, walking at quite a fast pace eager to get upstairs to the believer who had spoken to me of baptism and being saved. My heart sank at the moment, and I remembered he had been failing in health and had recently went on Hospice.

I was frightened to walk into his room and ask this man who had once asked me to let him know when I was ready to be baptized. I couldn't bring myself to knock on his door for several hours, but something within me was driving me, beyond my control. I went to his door, knocked, and entered. He recognized me and began talking immediately. I told him about my previous night and asked if he was still willing to baptize me.

The believer told me there wasn't much time. To my surprise, he sat straight up out of bed and began searching his phone for a nearby church with a pool. I was beyond mortified, as he had been in and out of consciousness and was nowhere near safe enough to leave the room let alone the building. I was quite panicked and went back down to the therapy room where I would then meet up with a Christian coworker whom I would submit my worries to about my earlier discussion with the believer. My coworker very calmly went upstairs, talked with this man, the believer, and made a plan to have me baptized. I remember my coworker coming up to me saying, "Let's go, you're getting baptized in his room today."

# Baptism

I have never been so excited and yet nervous at the same time as I was in that very moment. The time was 2:29 PM on that warm Fall day as was recorded by the wonderful man, the Believer who baptized me that day. The believer, whom I mentioned was quite frail and unconscious at times, was more alive and vibrant than ever. The believer seemed to gain strength when he talked of the Lord. He stood over me on his two feet as I sat in a chair with my back against the counter with my head in the sink as I was washed clean. The believer's words flowed from his mouth as if they had somehow been rehearsed, like he had known all along what he was to say. He baptized me in the name of Jesus Christ, and I felt what I can only explain as a higher power, supernatural of sorts, enter my body through my throat, which I instantly knew within me to be the power of the Holy Spirit. I knew with all certainty I was a child of God.

For those who are led by the Spirit of God are the children of God. The Spirit you received does not make you slaves, so that you live in fear again; rather, the Spirit you received brought about your adoption to sonship. And by him we cry, "Abba, Father. The Spirit himself testifies with our spirit that we are Gods children. (Rom. 8:14–16, NIV)

I could finally answer the previous question with no dispute on whether I knew or not whether I was going to heaven. My eyes were open for the first time, and what a glorious sight. I no longer looked to my past, I loved in a way I never quite knew existed. I cried the entire day, no exaggeration, I cried and cried and cried happy tears of joy the entire day. The Lord, who had given me these four beautifully stubborn children, had an awesome plan for me all along. My children, whom God had been preparing for me, had literally brought me to my knees! Thank you, Jesus! God, you are so good, you brought me to the storm only to pull me out of the storm at your perfect timing! Words cannot begin to explain the currents rushing through my veins that day, the blood of Jesus Christ.

Many times, people have told me over the years how I must be such a strong person for that God must have known I could handle my son with autism. I know now with all my heart the very opposite of that to be true. The very son that has challenged me to my very core could possibly be the very weapon the Lord needed to reach me. With each child that came into my life brought with it more stress, more difficulty, until finally bringing me to my knees asking for salvation! What an extraordinary gift from God, for his timing has been nothing short of perfect.

The day of my baptism was and is the most glorious day of my life. To know and feel complete unconditional love from the father above is like no other. There really are no words that can explain or capture this feeling. This really is something that cannot be understood until the moment you experience it for yourself.

The day following my baptism, I could hardly wait to run upstairs to the believer's room. Upon entering work for the day, I remember feeling so full of complete joy, happiness, and excitement. What an awesome high to be saved; I felt the Holy Spirit racing through my veins! I couldn't wait to share my joy with the believer who had a helping hand in bringing me along to this amazing moment in my life.

I felt the breathing seize in my lungs as I looked upon a man I had so much love for, who had just the day prior baptized me in his sink, but not a few feet from where I stood. I would never have another conversation with the believer, he would remain unresponsive till his final breath. I would like to think he knew I was in his room with him, praying with him, showing him the kindness, he had so freely given me at one time not so long ago. I had not one, but many days that would follow of sorrow that would be shared with close coworkers and the believer's family. I was fortunate enough to be alongside wonderful people at this delicate time who all gathered to celebrate the life of this wonderful man whom had all in one way or another touched our hearts.

For me, the reality of God's work was extremely prevalent. The believer, who had within twenty-four hours ago stood on his own two feet baptizing me in this very room, was now lying unresponsive to those around him.

The Lord had sent me a miracle. The believer was in my life at precisely the right moments right up until his last breath. Coincidence, I think not! How precise the Lord's work is, for each and every one of us he has a plan. If my story isn't proof of that, then I don't know what is.

The believer would pass away less than a week from the time he baptized me. What a rollercoaster of emotions I was on for the coming weeks. I would never speak or have just one more conversation with this amazing man. I'm not going to lie, the one person I wanted to speak with more than anyone at this time was none other than the believer. I was absolutely crushed to not have him by my side during this time. I am certain the believer was placed on my path by none other than the Lord above to nurture me on my journey to becoming a believer myself. I am in complete awe of the Lord and his amazing grace.

The believer will forever hold a very special place in my heart. He floods my thoughts daily in some form or another.

I am often reminded of the believer's kindness and love he had and shared for Jesus. I have never met a man quite as the believer. He reminds me a lot of Jesus's disciples who went about their lives spreading news of the Lord. For what some may simply call a drifter, others may call their messenger. He loved to talk and was extremely social. The believer's conversations always turned to Jesus regardless of whatever he may be talking about. Many times, I would return the believer back to his room following therapy and be shown on his computer his latest scripture reading he was studying, or he would hand me a copy of scripture he had come across that he thought I may like to read. I feel as if the believer was a messenger sent to me by none other than Jesus himself. For almost a year, the believer had been professing God's word to me and my family of coworkers. As I look back on my time with the believer and fellow coworkers, we all can plainly see how much closer each one of us came to one another and most of all the Lord.

My fellow coworkers and myself were changing, Jesus had become the main focus among each of us. I am very blessed to have had the opportunity to share my baptism and testimony with these amazing individuals. The Lord really does surround us with people to encourage us and help us on our journeys. My coworkers continue to help guide me on my faithful journey.

I've been asked a few times if I would ever be baptized again in a church or by a pastor. I honestly love that my baptism was perfectly imperfectly planned. Jesus was with me in the believer's tiny room on the third floor of the building that day. The believer was chosen to be the one to perform my baptism. Jesus performs miracles every day, anywhere, at any given time. I cannot think of a more perfect baptism. I am beyond honored the Lord chose this very story to be my testimony.

How through the years I have been seeking, dipping my toe in ever so slightly, only to pull back until finally through my children, through the work of the Lord I now see the light.

I'm made new. I'm changing, I'm singing a never-ending song of praise through the day. My children and husband are noticing I'm reading the Bible, being just a little gentler, showing love and kindness. Immediately following baptism, I'm headed back to church, the very church I have dipped my toe in and out of for eight years.

# Back to Church

Somehow, the doors to the church seemed much more inviting than I had once remembered. I felt alive for the first time. A few people recognized me even though I had not been there in nearly three years. I did not feel awkward or alone, like I had so many times before. I was greeted by a close friend whom I had known and loved for years. For God had been placing wonderful Christian people in my life for years, how did I not see this until now? The first person I called after being baptized was my friend, Alyssa, for I knew she would know the importance and complete joy that I was experiencing. She is a wonderful example of kindness and love, and she is a true gift in my life.

I had been gone from the church for quite some time but felt like I had found my comfort immediately upon my return. I was given a warm greeting by the people of the church and welcomed by the pastor's wife. My two oldest daughters joined me in my return to church that Sunday.

Both of my daughters had been to church prior but not consistently. My daughters both were very moved that day. I don't know if the credit goes to the great worship music or the presence of great Christians, but one thing is for certain, this would become the church my children would repeatedly ask to return to.

Week by week, I began bringing another one of my children through the doors of the church until all four were attending and participating in Sunday school classes. On the third week when finally, all four children came to church, I recall my husband sliding into the driver's seat of the car as I was fastening the last of the kid's car seat buckles. And then there were six, all family members accounted for! I remember wondering what some of the church members must have thought of me every week showing up with yet another child, wondering exactly how many children I must have, Ha.

What a wonderful day Sunday has become for my family. My husband and I have learned to cherish this childless hour of worship in the sanctuary as a time to draw close to one another while placing our faith in the Lord. I believe this very hour in my week helps to restore my soul and also reconnect with my husband without even saying a word as we sit hand in hand united. My four children have become very connected to the church in their own ways and look forward to attending Sunday school. My three-year-old daughter confided in me one Sunday morning that Sundays had become her favorite day of the week because she gets to go to God's house! What an amazing thing to hear as a parent! This same daughter of mine begged me to let her attend Sunday school classes versus being taken to the nursery. She later in the week came to me following her first Sunday school class informing me she had been visited by Jesus while attending class. She told me Jesus was wearing a purple robe and had long curly hair. She continued to tell me he had come in to check on her but did not stay long. My first thought was, *Wow, my daughter has quite the imagination!*

As the days passed, I continued to ponder this idea of Jesus visiting my three year old. Whether she actually saw Jesus, that is disputable; however, the very idea that she understands the concept that Jesus cares for her and watches over her is beautiful. At the raw age of three, she is interpreting her relationship with Jesus and setting the path of her life. She has given myself and others hope and comfort in the truth that Jesus walks amongst us. Children understand much more than we realize or give them credit for. Doesn't the Bible tell us this very thing?

I began to see all of my children drawing nearer not only to the church, but the Lord. Many questions have been brought up on several occasions regarding heaven, the meaning of being saved, and Jesus's love for us. To think that just shy of a few months prior my children did not have any of this in their lives or myself for that matter is nothing short of amazing. My children are beginning to sing songs of worship throughout the day, even my young three-year-old is singing words of praise! My son, Noah, is allowing Christian music to be played in the house and in the car! He still has a hard time dealing with noises and a variety of different sounds, especially when in crowded places. Many times, at church I will look over and notice Noah covering his ears. Usually a gentle touch and soothing words are enough to calm him. His mouth; however, is not always as easy to tame unfortunately!

My life is not the only one that is being changed. But things started with just one change in one person. Wow, how amazing! I try not to think of what may have been or could have happened in my children's lives if I had not been saved. May the Lord work in me and all his children for the advancement of his kingdom. Our actions really do affect other people.

I am fortunate enough to have the opportunity to speak of God's truth and pray with my patients at work. I see all walks of life, all ages coming for rehabilitation with many different diagnoses. Many times, I am seeing people at their worst. Patients come from the hospital after surgery, traumatic accident, or life-threatening experiences. Not every day is easy for the patient or for myself for that matter. I do care a great deal for my patients and tend to become their cheerleader during their times of need. This also gives me a chance to talk about the Lord when people may be at a low point or facing hard times with their health.

Prayers for recovery and encouragement to keep trying and moving forward is so very important at these times. For every patient that I see that has amazing family support, I also see with little to no support from loved ones. Many have no children or family in the area. Becoming older can be extremely difficult, lonely, and depressing for some. I'd like to think God has placed me in the work field I am in to be a messenger for those in need. Therapy has become so much more to me than just a profession. Yes, I do my job I was taught in school, but I also get to be so much more for my patients.

I am so very fortunate to work alongside other caring Christians who share my love for the Lord. We are a family, we are more than just a place of employment, we love our residents, and we hurt when they hurt. Many times, we have held hands of those that we know are not going to survive the day. We get to speak of Jesus, our savior, bringing news of redemption to those in need. I'm learning to be a vehicle for God's will. I am far from perfect, and on more than one occasion, I have been known to have a bad day. Politics of the job are not always fun or easy to deal with, therefore making my job stressful at times.

God sustains me and strengthens me in all seasons and times of my life. I continue to need the Lord every week, every day, and every hour. I am well aware that I need the Lord to carry me through. I have a very busy life as does everyone else that can be very demanding and draining. The Lord sees me through.

I am nowhere near perfect. I continue to struggle, with mornings especially. I find myself at God's mercy daily to get me through. Daily prayers to give me strength, understanding, compassion, and yes, patience go up consistently. I can get through any day because, and only because, Jesus is my savior.

Recently, during church, my two youngest children began misbehaving and fighting over my attention. I felt the fear of gossip creep upon me worried about what the others around me may be thinking of my children and my parenting. At one point, I looked over at my son, and he had a glow stick hanging from his nose. I felt quite mortified. As I yanked the glow stick from my son's nose, it hit me, surely other parents and grandparents have been through these behaviors with their own children. Just maybe others do understand and are not necessarily sitting here pointing fingers at me. I am learning that fear comes in many forms. We are people not measuring sticks to be compared.

> Do not judge, or you too will be judged. For in the same way you judge others, you will be judged, and with the measure you use, it will be measured to you. (Matt. 7:1–3, NIV)

We all go through trials and difficult times, and we continue to be transformed and to grow. I know one of my personal weaknesses is my patience. I've got four pretty good reminders who keep me in check daily! I tend to stress and worry far more than I should. I am learning to let go and only worry about the day at hand.

> Therefore do not worry about tomorrow, for tomorrow will worry about itself. Each day has enough trouble of its own. (Matt. 7:34, NIV)

# Freedom

Belief in Jesus equals freedom. I have never felt free until the day my eyes were open. The Lord gives us freedom to love and be loved like no other. I am free to love my kids, husband, and family like I have always dreamed of. Are there tough times? Yes.

I have always heard the phrase, "You can't love others until you learn to love yourself." I did not learn to love myself until I knew the love of Jesus. God chose me, he chooses us, and he created us. There really is no need to be someone other than who we are designed to be, for he already designed us perfectly. I don't need to try to be someone I'm not because I have the one and only acceptance I need.

How foolish I have been through the years thinking if I looked this way or that I would be liked more or accepted. The Lord knows very well what I look like and what I was designed to look like for he is and was the very creator of my being. Being a Christian is such an amazing feeling. Just knowing that God loves us so much that he gave his only son for us is beyond comprehension. How our God can continue to love us through all of our failures and self-ishness, through the deep and sometimes dark feelings that are stored away in our hearts; God knows it all and still continues to love us.

For God so loved the world that he gave his
one and only son, that whoever believes in
him shall not perish but have eternal life.
(John 3:16, NIV)

With becoming a believer also comes with it, Satan's increase awareness. I became very much aware of Satan trying to gain a foothold in my life after becoming a believer. I remember one morning waking, feeling like someone was literally attacking me through the entire night. This left me feeling numb, fatigued, and extremely irritable. Random thoughts, past sins, and events would haunt my dreams through the night.

I have learned to pray and ask for protection to keep Satan from me and my family. Satan is very sneaky and hides in the darkness ready to pounce at any opportunity or situation that presents itself. I am learning to keep my shield of armor close as well as on at all times from the dark one. I'm learning to control myself; however, I am also learning how Satan is able to use others around me to make attempts at me. Personally, this is the hardest for me. Satan is able to stir up anger in others in order to plot against us in hopes we will slip from grace. I am trying to be prepared at all times to fight the battle of Satan that continues when least expecting it, in whatever form that may take on.

We all sin, and we are not perfect. God's grace, the very act of Jesus on the cross, saves us. Being a believer and relying on Jesus is what grounds me. I always try to remember on my worst and challenging days that this is not my home, but a place I am in for a short time. Heaven is our ultimate destination, our everlasting promise from above.

Looking back throughout my past years, I am now able to see many of the moments Jesus was trying to reach me. Certain people had been placed in my path friends, coworkers, children, and certain situations that had to be none other than the Lord's work. It's amazing how many attempts and try's the Lord is willing to give us, and how willing he is to continue to fight for our salvation. I continue to be in complete awe and amazement of our God. I now understand why the Lord chose the name Noah for our son. For the Lord sent this child, my son to save me from the disastrous flood of my life. I continue to pray for my children and family members that they may all come to know the Lord and accept Jesus as their savior. How sad is it that people may take their last breath never accepting Jesus into their lives? Now that I have been forgiven, I cannot even begin to fathom a life without Jesus. Such important work we are here to do. We have been chosen to be the light of the world, and what a great honor. My hope is that I may be able to fulfill whatever it is the Lord has in store for me. I pray to always have a heart willing to listen and receive Jesus's words with arms open wide to further God's kingdom.

For you were once darkness, but now you
are light in the Lord. (Eph. 5:8, NIV)

I often wonder about my son, who has autism, and how he will come to know Jesus. A very wise person once told me, "God created your son with autism, knowing exactly what he is capable of"! I believe with all my heart for that to be true. God does not make mistakes. For the Lord is the one who created my son, then obviously he must know how to reach him! I am learning to put my trust in the Lord. I trust the Lords judgement over my own, nor do I want to be in control. It is quite freeing to know the Lord has things under control. I am not wise or full of the answers like the Lord is. How much more freeing it is to realize I wake up and just ask the Lord to guide me. When I attempt to take control of a situation, the stress comes rolling in and things start tearing apart at the seams. Jesus reminds us all too well that we need him and are not capable of handling things on our own. What a relief to know that we can find rest in the Lord. I am far from perfect and I find myself clinging to the Lord. The one thing I know in this life to be true is the Lord. I am thankful for not having it all together, and even more thankful for a loving and kind savior that knows what I need before asking it.

> Come to me, all you who are weary and burdened, and I will give you rest. Take my yoke upon you and learn from me, for I am gentle and humble in heart, and you will find rest for your souls. For my yoke is easy and my burden is light. (Matt. 11:28–30, NIV)

This is one of my favorite scriptures in the Bible. I am reminded of this passage often, and continue to be drawn to its message.

This book I am writing may never be a best seller, or even published, or may actually just be intended for my children and family to read one day. I am driven to write so; therefore, I will write. What the Lord has in store for this manuscript I do not know. It is his to do with at his will.

Shortly after becoming saved, God placed on my heart that I was to write a book. Now I fought the idea of writing and struggled with this task for awhile. I've wondered if maybe I was misunderstanding him. I remember while driving to work one day having this constant vision of a book. I was given a name during my thoughts of this book title. As I started my work day, I decided to actually write down this title because this name must be important if I continued to keep running it through my mind. So, I wrote the name down, and later decided to look this title up of what I assumed must be a book on the internet. I thought, well, maybe the Lord is instructing me to read something that may help me on my journey. The title was nowhere to be found, nor was it a book. I tried to ignore the notion of writing a book, but it just kept coming back to me. So, here I am, writing this book, which I believe to be 100 percent of the Lord's doing.

I pray that whatever reason I am to be writing this, that I am giving justice to God's words. I pray that whoever may read this may come to have hope and faith in the Lord our savior. All glory is through the Lord's work on this project. The Lord is driving, I am just the passenger. Although, I will say seeing the Lord's words from my thoughts come to life on paper is pretty amazing. I am still very emotional with my testimony and have often struggled with the thought of wanting to keep it to myself. I have had moments of weakness with the fear of others views that may come from my story; however, the Lord is continuing to lead me forward. My faith surpasses any fears I may possibly have. I feel beyond blessed to have come to have a personal relationship with Jesus. I am forever grateful for the wonderful people who have come into my life at just the right time to guide me on my spiritual journey.

I continue to have struggles in life, and that is where hope in the Lord frees me. I do not believe perfect contentment on earth is possible for a believer; however, I know that surviving on earth is possible with Jesus.

I do not know what the future holds for me; nevertheless, I am content with the here and now. I am trying to enjoy every minute I can with my children and family. I am trying to focus on the moments at hand versus the future— mainly because I do not know what the future entails or what that will look like. Honestly, I'm not sure I necessarily want to know ahead of time. As I've learned, God leads me to where he needs me or wants me to be. I trust he knows what's best for me.

I often wonder what the future holds for my four children. I think about how Jesus will reach each and every one of them. If I get to teach my children one thing in this world, I hope it is that they may know Jesus as their savior. When we get right down to it, that's really all that matters.

Jesus answered, "I am the way and the
truth and the life. No one comes to the
Father except through me." (John 14:6,
NIV)

I often think of the years ahead of me where I will
see my children struggling or heading the wrong direction.
Such a scary vision for a parent. I am praying now for what
may be to come. We live in a scary and vicious world where
we are unable to shield our children from the horrifying
things around us. Fear for our children can consume a parent. Jesus is the only one who can save our children. I pray
that I give my children every chance to know, love, and
accept Jesus into their lives.

My thoughts often flood to Noah and what the future
may hold for him. I am very excited to continue to see
him grow and mature. He has been such a blessing and an
amazing miracle to watch blossom. I feel amazing things
are going to happen for him. I completely trust the Lord
has a great plan and will make a way for my son in this
crazy world we live in.

Not so long ago, I spent too much time worrying about
my son's future and where that would lead me as well into
my future. What a waste of my energy! I do not control my
future any more than I control my son's future. Will Noah
be sufficient enough to live and work on his own? Will I
need to become his caregiver? The questions could go on
and on. I do know that my son was non-verbal at one time
and now speaks. God has chosen when to unveil Noah's

gifts, and how special and in complete awe we are watching Noah achieve what we never knew was possible.

I look forward to seeing the gifts the Lord has in store for our special son and all of our children. Children really are such a blessing from above. As a parent, the love we have for our children is so powerful. How much more powerful is God's love for us then! We often forget how very loved we are from above. For even the love we feel for our children does not come close to the love the Lord has for our very selves. I leave the Lord to watch over my children while I am at work for the day. What better watch guard than the Lord himself. As much as we want to keep tabs on our children at all times, there comes a time when you have to set them free in their own lives. It's scary as a parent to worry about the safety of our children. Casting our worries at Jesus's feet and diligent prayer for keeping our children safe is what keeps me sane.

The Lord has specifically designed each and every one of us. I am confident in the life the Lord has prepared for my family and myself. I do not have all of the answers, as do none of us. The answer lies in Jesus.

For the readers who may be seeking or unsure…it's never too late to call upon Jesus. We never know when our last days on earth will come. I can assure you the life you have is nothing compared to the life you can have through Jesus Christ. "In the time of my favor I hear you, and in the day of salvation I helped you" "I tell you, now is the time of God's favor, now is the day of salvation." (Corinthians 6:1-2)

# Acknowledgments

First and foremost, I thank the Lord above for giving me his wisdom and insight for creating this book. Thank you, Lord for not giving up on me and encouraging me through this entire process; for giving me the words when my slate was blank. Thank you, Lord for moving mountains for a dream I never knew existed! I am in such complete amazement and am completely humbled by your power and love. I am your servant, lead me to wherever that may be...

Thank you, Covenant publishing for accepting the roughest of drafts, for believing in my work, and guiding me through this amazing adventure every step of the way.

# Doxology

To him who is able to keep you from stumbling and to present you before his glorious presence without fault and with great joy-to the only God our Savior be glory, majesty, power, and authority, through Jesus Christ our Lord, before all ages, now and forevermore! Amen. (Jude 25:24–25, NIV)

"Blessed are those who die in the Lord," says the Spirit of God. "Their work is done. Their trials are over. But their influence follows on long afterward." (Rev. 14:13, NIV)

In memory of the Believer, whom will always hold a special place in my heart. Thank you, faithful servant for your work in the Lord and your assistance setting me on my path of righteousness. I eagerly look forward to the day of embracing you once again.

Thank you to my wonderful husband Brad for being patient and allowing me the time to write among the business of our walls. Thank you, Brad for loving me during my times of Chaos trying to balance life while writing, for understanding how important it has been for me to complete this task. I am blessed beyond measure to have you for a husband and each and every one of our beautiful children. I can not wait to see what the Lord has in store for us.

To my children, you will never know how dearly I love each and every one of you. You are my greatest blessings in life. May you all call upon Jesus and be saved. Mama loves you!

Thank you to my wonderful parents and family for their unconditional love. My mother, for always being my listening ear and my rock in life. Thank you for taking the time to listen to my ideas and review my work prior to sharing it. I am blessed to call you both my parents.

Thank you to my grandmother for showing me her dedication as well as her relationship through the years with the Lord. You have been a constant reminder of Jesus' love through your beautiful ways in life.

Thank you to my coworkers Betsy and Greg you are like family to me. Thank you, for being a part of the most important day of my life. My heart holds both of you close. The Lord sure knew what he was doing when he brought the three of us together! "Peace be Still" Mark 4:39 (NIV)

Thank you, Alyssa for being such a caring friend and encouraging me through my process of writing. Thank you for being my listening ear, my voice of reason, and continuing to pray for me and my family through our life trials.

Thank you, Rosalie for being our Saving Grace and loving our son. I am beyond words…how very grateful I am to you for everything you do.

Thank you to all the wonderful teachers, instructors, and therapists who have worked with my son and continue to make a difference in our lives. We are forever grateful.

Thank you, to the Alliance church for welcoming my family into your church with open arms.

To the beautiful and courageous women in my life who are fighting the battle of cancer, I lift my heart and prayers to you.

"And in their prayers for you their hearts will go out to you, because of the surpassing grace God has given you, Thanks be to God for his indescribable gift!" Corinthians 9:14-15 (NIV)

# References

NIV Quest Study Bible.
Edited by Marshall Shelley, et al.
Grand Rapids, Michigan; Zondervan, 2011

(http://www.aocd.org)
(Behindthename.com)

# About the Author

Juliana Clark is an occupational therapy assistant, COTA/L. She received an associate's degree of science from Owens Community College of Toledo. Juliana and her husband, Brad, have four children and live in Ohio where they attend an Alliance Church.

Printed in the USA
CPSIA information can be obtained
at www.ICGtesting.com
LVHW042259180324
774778LV00004B/294